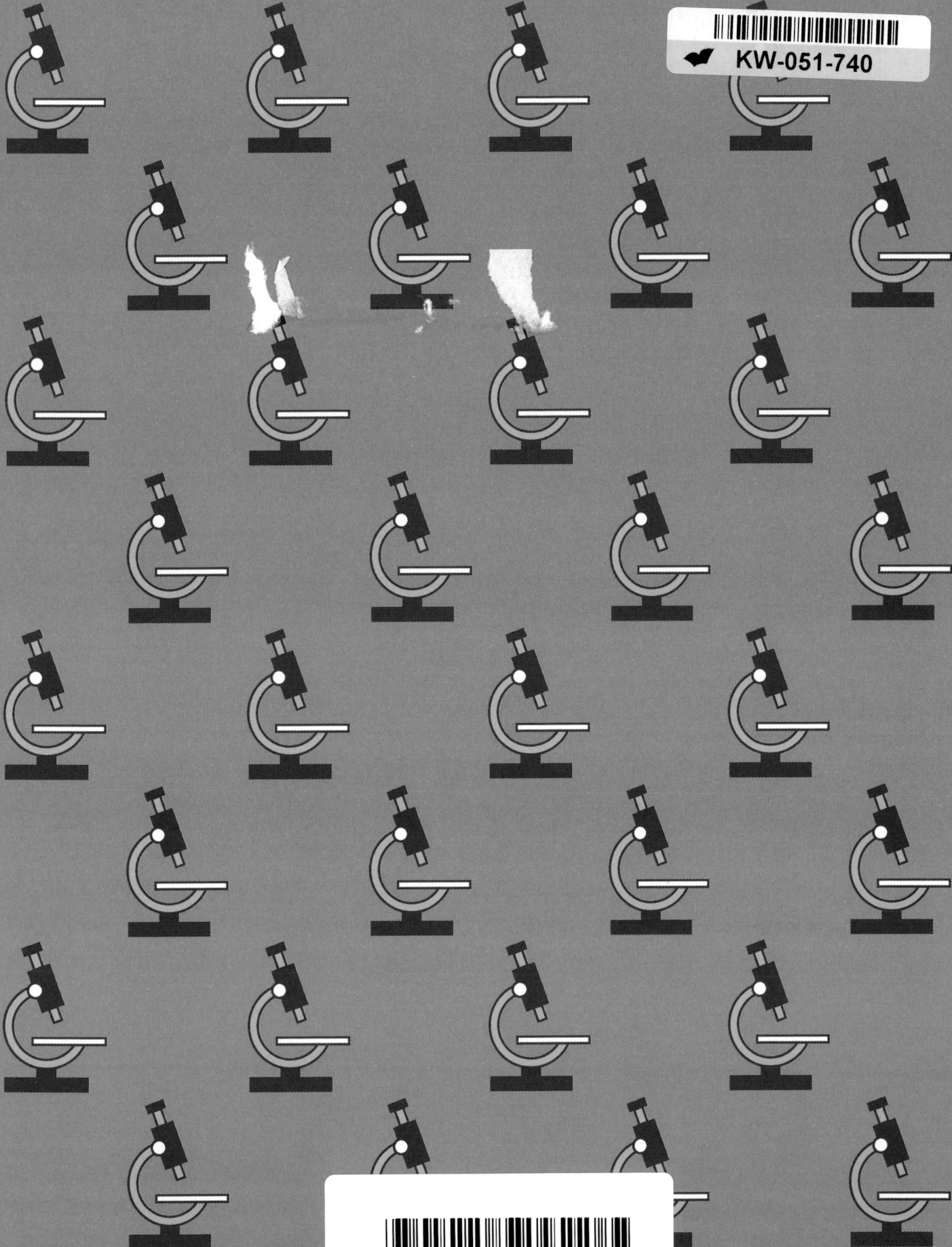

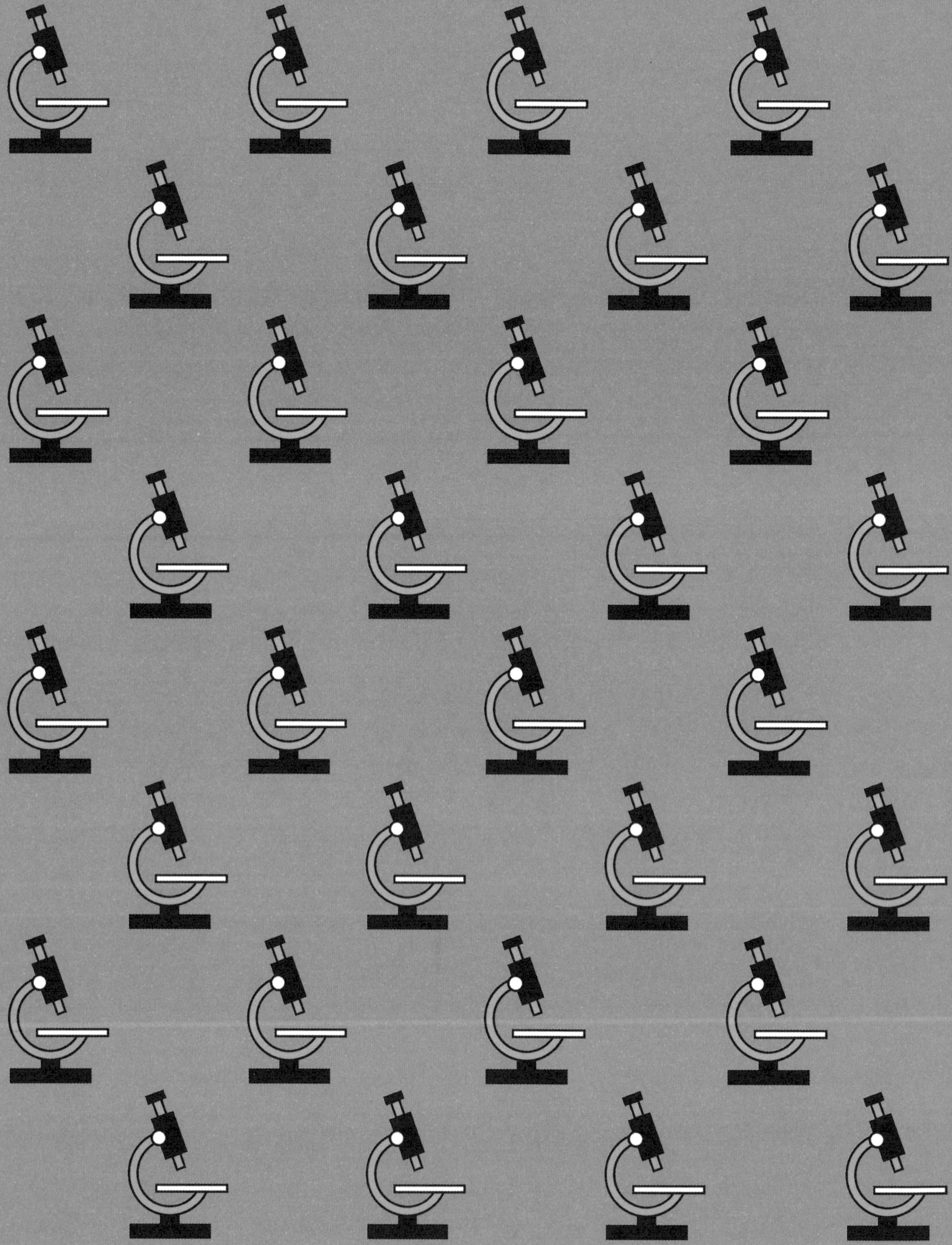

MICROSCOPIC CREATURES

ZOOM IN ON DIATOMS, TARDIGRADES, PLANKTON AND MUCH MORE!

WAYLAND

Anna Claybourne

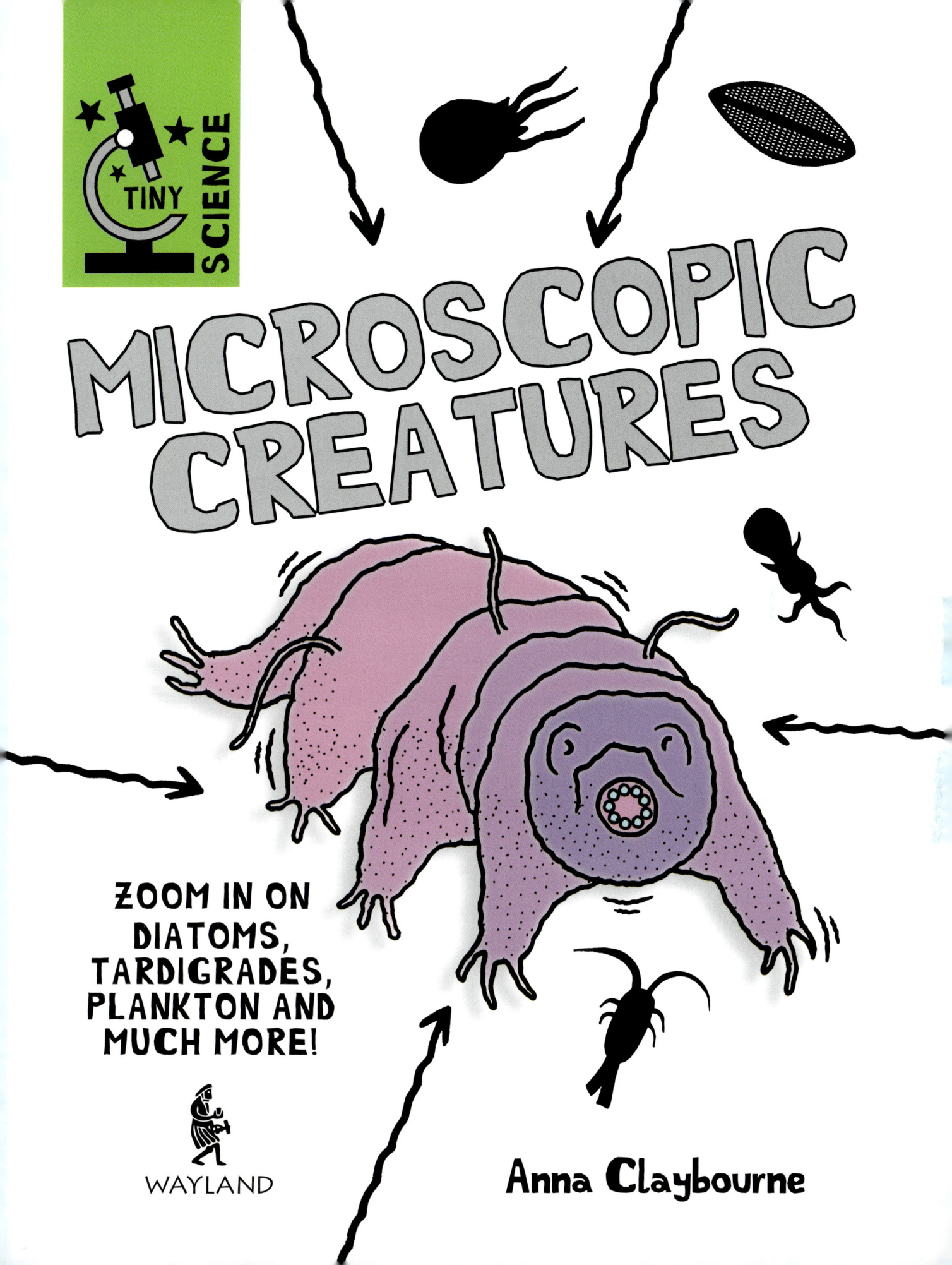

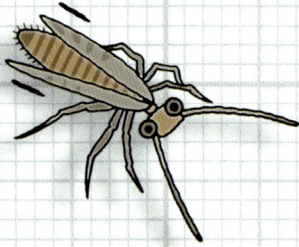

First published in Great Britain in 2022
by Wayland

© Hodder and Stoughton, 2022

Credits:
Editor: Grace Glendinning
Design and illustrations: Matt Lilly
Cover design: Matt Lilly

ISBN hb 978 1 5263 1787 2
ISBN pb 978 1 5263 1788 9

Printed and bound in China

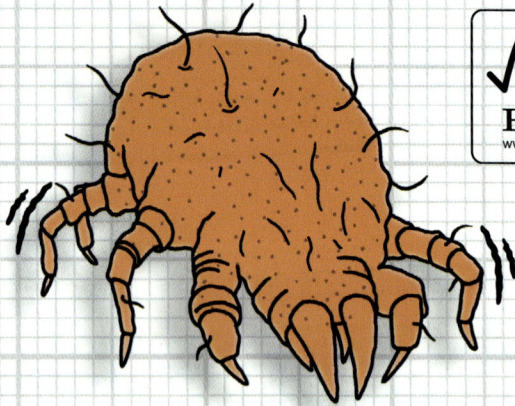

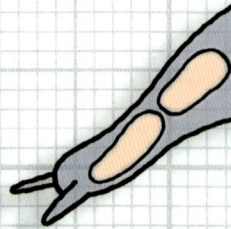

MIX
Paper from
responsible sources
FSC
www.fsc.org
FSC® C104740

Picture credits:

Alamy: Nigel Cattlin 27t; Hum Images 11t;Phanie 25b; Science Photo Library 23t.
Getty Images: Oxford Scientific 18.
Flickr: Stefan Siebert 19c.
NASA: 6c.
Science Photo Library: Wim Van Egmond 15tl;
Steve Gschmeissner 14c, 20b, 22br; Power & Syred 20c, 31b.
Shutterstock: Peddalanka Ramesh Babu 13bl, 17t; Choksawatdikorn 15tr, 17bl;
Dan4Earth 21c; Funny angel 16t;Gallinago media 17bc; HHelene 17cl;
Image Source Trading Ltd 7b;C Jansuebsri 17cr; Kateryna Kon 4b, 16c, 22cl, 27b;
Henri Koskinen 19b; Alex Manders 24b;Rdonar 21t; Arunee Rodloy 8; Sciencepics 9br, 14t;
SciePro 5tl, 23c; 3drenderings 27c; 3Dstock 4c, 12b; Sergey Vladmirov 19t.
Wellcome Collection/CCA.4.0 International 6b, 7c.
Wikimedia Commons: NOAA/PD 9bl; Christopher Pooley, USDA-ARS 5tr; Jeroen
Rouwkema 7t; Zookeys 10t/ Dr Barna Páll-Gergely and Nikolett Szpisjak 26t.

Every effort has been made to clear copyright.
Should there be any inadvertent omission, please apply
to the publisher for rectification

Wayland
An imprint of
Hachette Children's Group
Part of Hodder and Stoughton
Carmelite House
50 Victoria Embankment
London EC4Y 0DZ

An Hachette UK Company
www.hachette.co.uk
www.hachettechildrens.co.uk

Contents

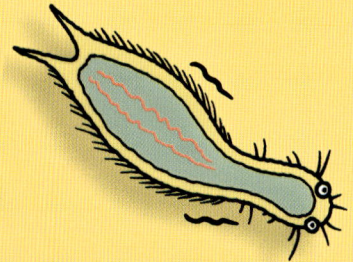

Tiny life

On Planet Earth, we're surrounded by millions of living things …

BZZZZ!

Grass, trees, flowers, pets, birds, insects, bears, sharks, lizards, whales … all kinds of things!

MIAOW!

HELLOOO! THERE'S MORE ABOUT ME ON PAGE 12!

But did you know that most of the living things all around us are actually **INVISIBLE?!** Not because they're magic – but because they're too small to see, such as this tiny tardigrade!

Micro-life

There are thousands of species, or types, of these tiny creatures, which scientists call microorganisms. Microorganisms include living things that have only one cell, like bacteria, archaea and yeast.

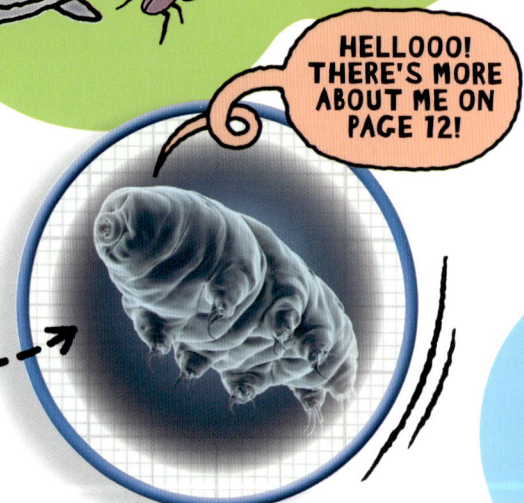

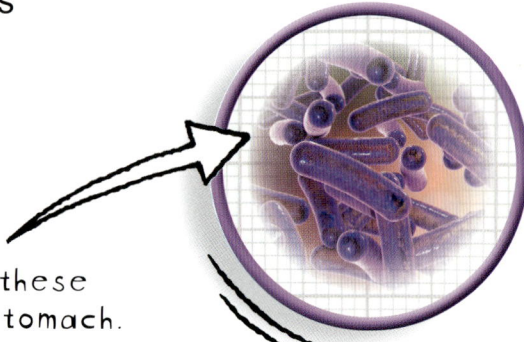

Under the microscope

Bacteria sometimes cause diseases, like these Shigella bacteria, which cause an upset stomach.

There are also microscopic plants, teeny-weeny insects and spiders, and many other micro-sized animals. Some are pests, and some are harmless. Sometimes they live in our homes, and even on or **INSIDE** our bodies.

This could be living in your house ... but don't worry! It won't bite you.

I COME IN PEACE!

And sometimes they're amazingly beautiful, like this peacock mite.

BEST IN SHOW

How small is too small to see?

It depends on how good your eyesight is, but the smallest objects most people can see are around 0.1 mm across. That's one tenth of a millimetre, or the thickness of a human hair.

To measure tiny things, scientists use micrometres, or

μm.

One micrometre is one thousandth of a millimetre.

The peacock mite on this page is about 100 μm long.

A human hair is between 50 and 200 μm wide.

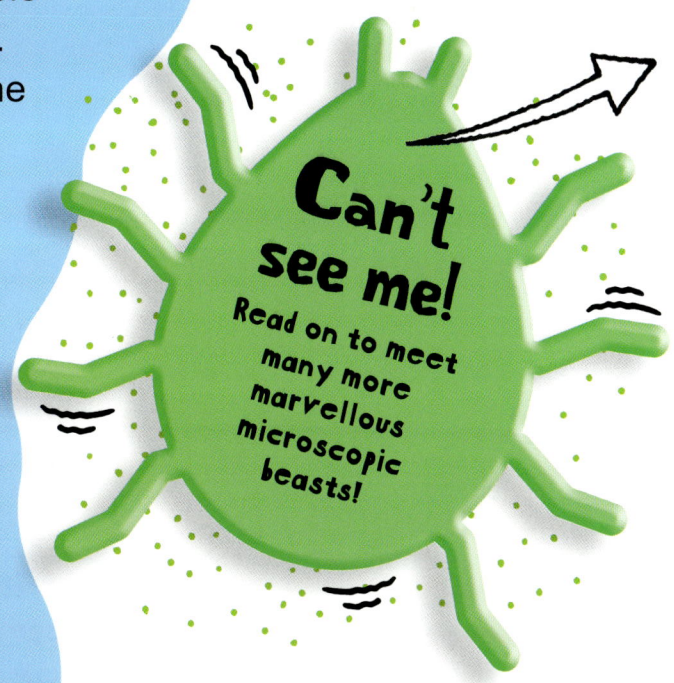

Can't see me!

Read on to meet many more marvellous microscopic beasts!

A whole new world

For most of history, we couldn't see microorganisms, because there weren't any microscopes! We had no idea about the world of micro-beasts all around us.

The first microscopes

No one knows who first used tubes containing curved glass lenses to magnify objects. But by about 1610, people were using them regularly to look up-close at fleas and other creepy-crawlies.

The great scientist Galileo experimented with a basic microscope.

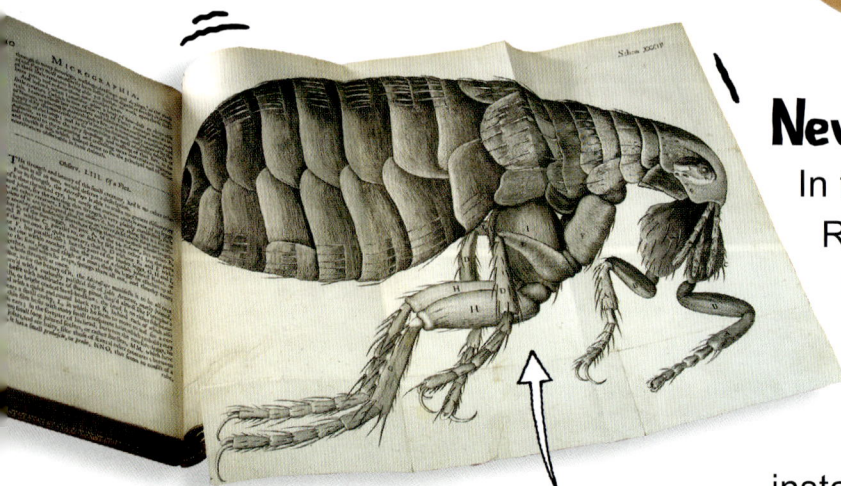

AMAZING!

New discoveries

In the 1660s, British scientist Robert Hooke used a microscope to study insects and plants. He published a book of close-up drawings of what he saw, called *Micrographia*. It was an instant bestseller!

Hooke's close-up drawing of a flea

And in the 1670s, Dutch inventor Antonie van Leeuwenhoek invented a much more powerful microscope, using a tiny glass ball as a lens.

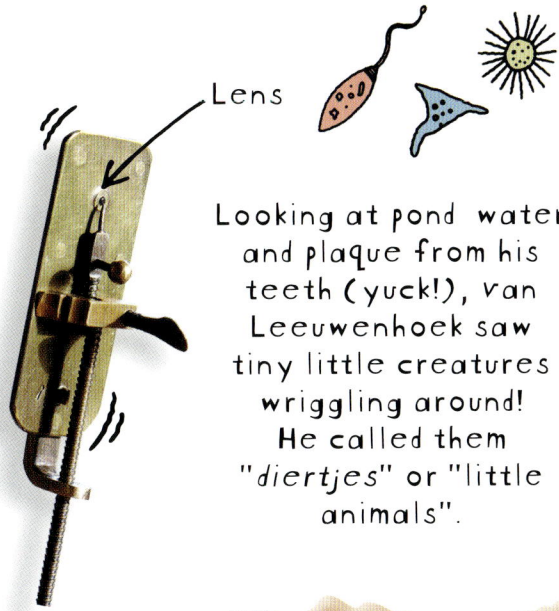

Lens

Looking at pond water and plaque from his teeth (yuck!), van Leeuwenhoek saw tiny little creatures wriggling around! He called them "*diertjes*" or "little animals".

Microscopes opened up a whole new world of science, helping us to understand germs and diseases, and the tiny cells that living things are made of.

Micro craze

By the 1800s, microscopes were easier to make, and many people could afford their own. There was a craze for looking at anything and everything through a microscope!

This cartoon from 1828 shows a woman being horrified by what she can see in a drop of river water!

Modern microscopes

Super-powerful modern microscopes use a beam of tiny particles called electrons to sense objects. They were used to capture a lot of the microscope images in this book.

Tiny plants

The plant family includes some of the world's biggest living things, like the towering giant sequoia tree.

Biggest plant

But you don't hear so much about the smallest plants. What are they like?

The smallest flowers

The smallest plant is Wolffia duckweed. When a pond looks all flat and green, as if you could walk across it, that's duckweed! It's made up of millions of tiny, ball-shaped plants floating on the water surface.

Each Wolffia is about the size of a cake sprinkle, so they are not actually microscopic, but their flowers are.

Smallest plant

Under the microscope

The teeny Wolffia flower

HELLO! I'M DOWN HERE!

Weeny seeds

The tiniest seeds, however, come from orchid plants. A single orchid seed pod can contain 4 million seeds! When the pod opens, they float out on the breeze like dust. In a few species, such as some types of jewel orchid, the individual seeds are too small to see without a microscope.

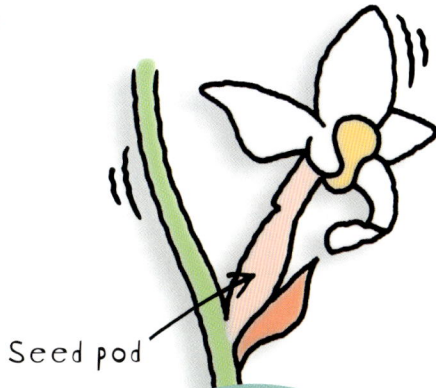

Seed pod

This jewel orchid's seeds are 10 μm (0.01 mm) wide and 50 μm (0.05 mm) long.

Single-celled algae

Even tinier are the single-celled algae, such as Chlorella and diatoms, usually found in water. They used to be included in the plant family, but now scientists class them as a separate group. Like plants, they are green and use energy from the sun to make food.

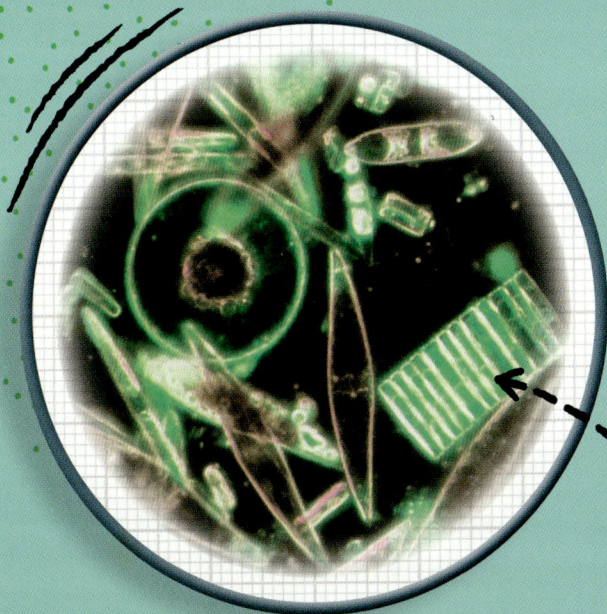

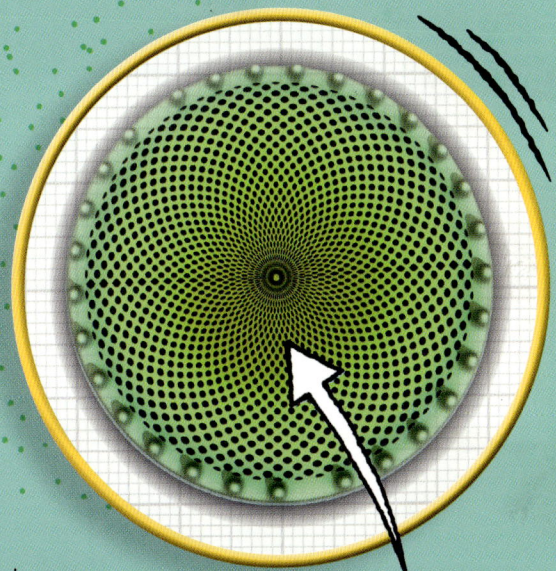

Diatoms: From 2 to 200 μm across

Chlorella: Up to 10 μm across

Tiny animals

Say hello to some of the world's tiniest animals!

Mini insects

The smallest insect is a tiny fairy fly. But it's not a fairy, and it's not a fly! It's actually a type of wasp.

Adult male fairy flies are only about 180 µm long – less than 0.2 mm (although the females are a bit bigger). They live inside the eggs of another insect, the bark louse.

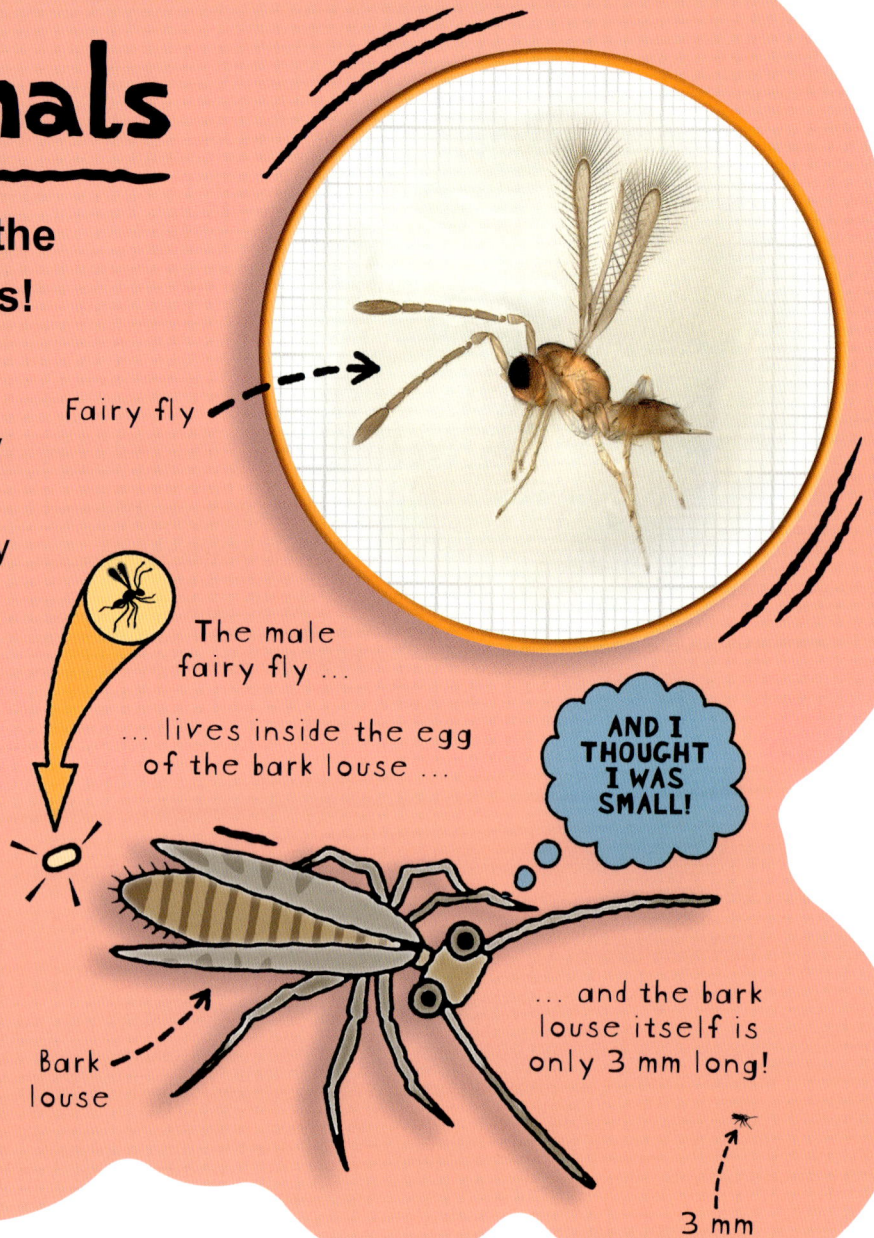

Fairy fly

The male fairy fly ...

... lives inside the egg of the bark louse ...

AND I THOUGHT I WAS SMALL!

Bark louse

... and the bark louse itself is only 3 mm long!

3 mm

Tiny spiders

The smallest known spiders are patu spiders, which can be as little as 0.4 mm long. They also build the tiniest webs, which can be just 1 cm across!

IF I WAS THIS BIG I'D SCARE MYSELF!

Spider actual size!

Web

Patu spider

However, spider relatives called mites are even smaller. Many are microscopic, like this palm mite, which feeds on coconut and banana plants.

SLURP!

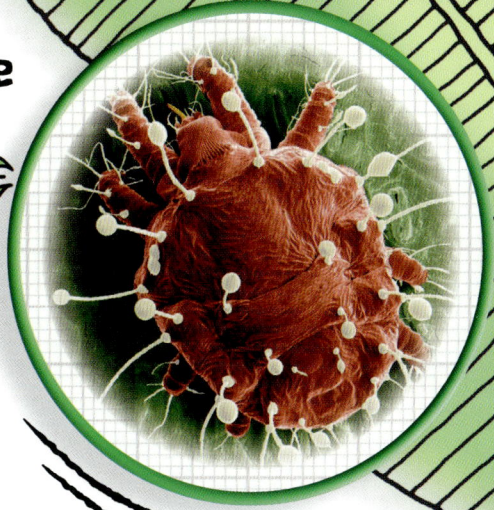

Palm mite ---->

Pond life

Pond water is full of tiny animals, as Antonie van Leeuwenhoek discovered when he tried out his home-made microscope (see page 7). Here are some of the creatures he could have seen ...

Rotifers
or "wheel animals" have parts on their heads that look like wheels.

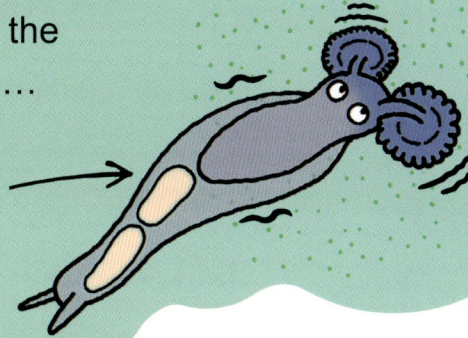

Gastrotrichs
(meaning "hairy bellies") are worm-shaped and hairy-looking.

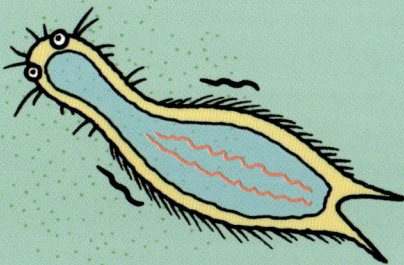

Daphnia
(or water fleas) are related to crabs and shrimps.

Pond dipping

If you want to try it yourself, you'll need a pond, an adult to help you and a simple microscope (or just a strong magnifying glass).

Use a jar or plastic container to catch some pond water.

Always make sure you have secure footing when pond dipping at the edge of the water.

Pour it on to a plain white tray or plate and take a look ...

11

Tiny but tough tardigrades

Tardigrades get these two pages all to themselves – because they're so amazing. As well as super-cute!

What are they?

Tardigrades are tiny animals with eight legs and a squishy-looking snout. They are invertebrates, like insects and spiders, but they are quite unlike any other animal.

Under the microscope

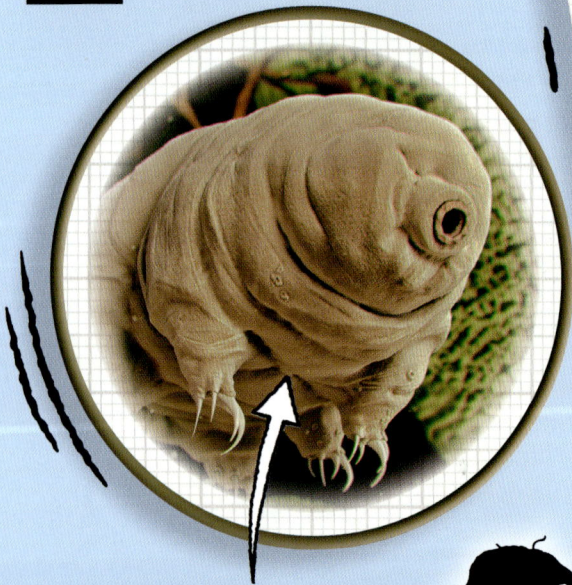

A microscope photo of a tardigrade on some moss

Tardigrade fact file

SIZE: Most are from 300–500 μm long (0.3–0.5 mm)

DIET: Plant juice, algae, bacteria and sometimes other tardigrades!

VARIETY OF SPECIES: Around 1,300

Tardigrades are everywhere!

Tardigrades prefer to live in watery or damp places, but they can survive almost anywhere. They've been found in …

- Moss and other plants
- High mountain tops
- The deep sea bed
- Antarctic ice
- Hot springs
- Stone walls
- Sand
- Soil
- And mud.

Piglets and bears

Some people think tardigrades look a bit like eight-legged bears or pigs, so they are nicknamed "water bears" or "moss piglets". "Tardigrades" means "slow-steppers", as the scientist who discovered them saw them walking very slowly.

Super-survivors

They may be slow, but tardigrades are probably the toughest animals on Earth. They can survive extreme heat and cold (from –272 °C to 151 °C), starvation, drying out and even dangerous nuclear radiation.

To get through tough times, a tardigrade pulls in its legs and head, and becomes a "tun", a tiny, dried-out ball. In this state, it can survive without food or water for over ten years!

A tardigrade tun

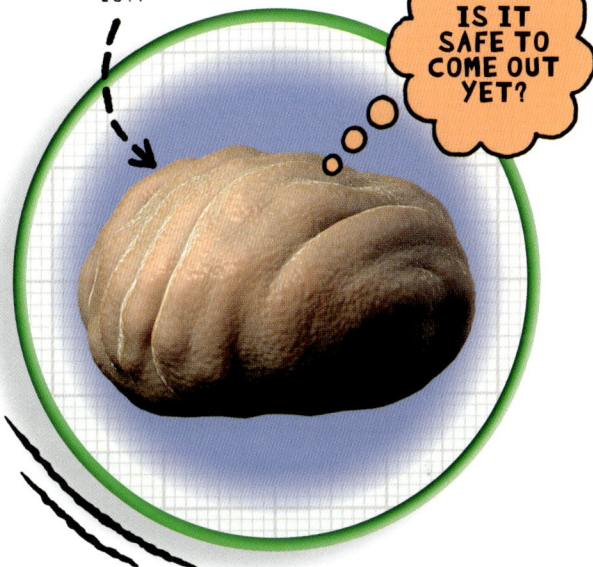

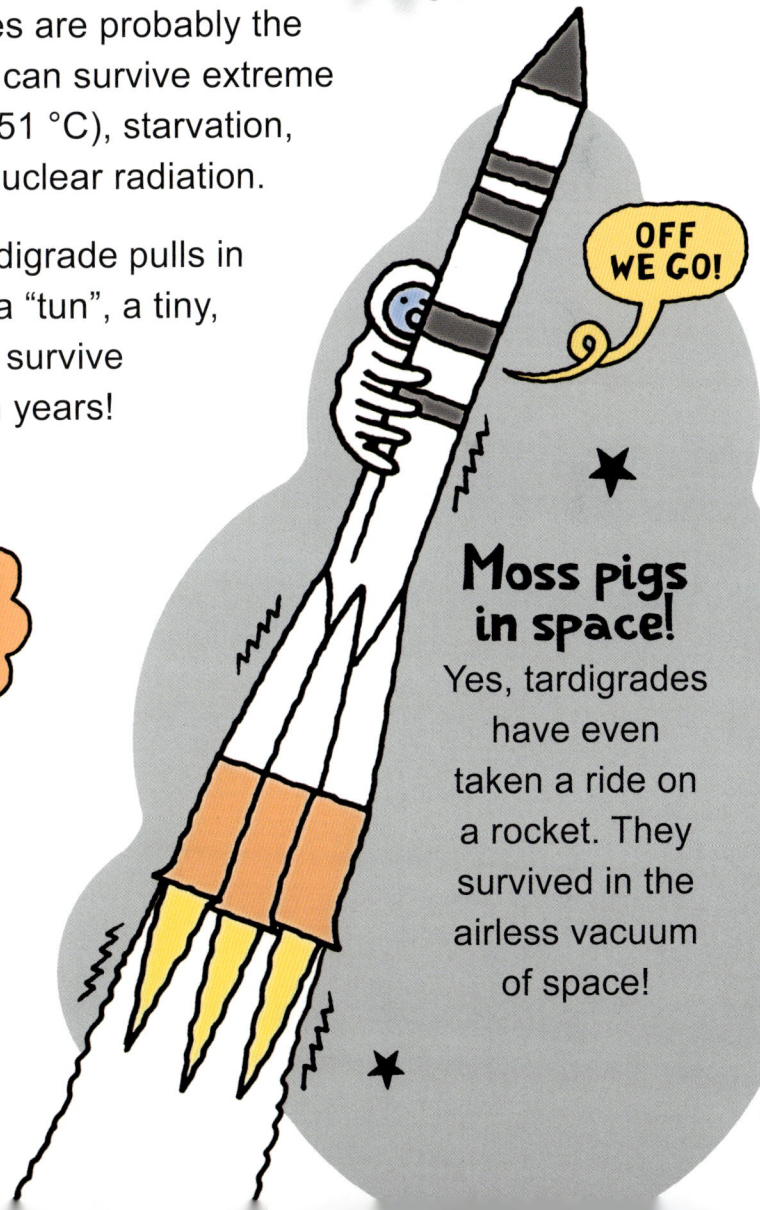

IS IT SAFE TO COME OUT YET?

OFF WE GO!

Moss pigs in space!

Yes, tardigrades have even taken a ride on a rocket. They survived in the airless vacuum of space!

Underwater world

Floating around in the upper layers of the oceans are trillions and trillions of tiny creatures, known as plankton. They're mostly microscopic, and incredibly important!

What is plankton?

Plankton aren't a particular type or species of living thing. Instead, they're a huge mixture of many different tiny creatures, drifting around together in the water.

Dinoflagellate

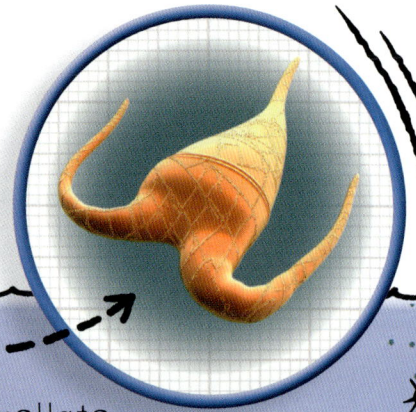

Plant-like plankton

Some plankton, called phytoplankton, work like plants, soaking up sunlight and using it to grow. They include tiny green algae, diatoms and other types, like these.

Coccolithophore, a type of single-celled plankton with a hard shell

Trees of the sea

Phytoplankton do another important job. Like forests on land, they soak up carbon dioxide gas from the air, and give out oxygen gas. This reduces global warming, and helps animals to breathe.

Bright lights at night

Some plankton are bioluminescent, meaning they can glow with their own light. They do this when they're disturbed, to try to put off predators. Sometimes this gives the sea a beautiful bluish glow.

Animal-like plankton

Plankton called zooplankton feed on the phytoplankton, or on one another. Zooplankton include tiny animals like copepods and forams, as well as the larvae (or babies) of larger sea creatures, such as jellyfish and sea stars.

Copepod, a kind of tiny shrimp-like sea creature

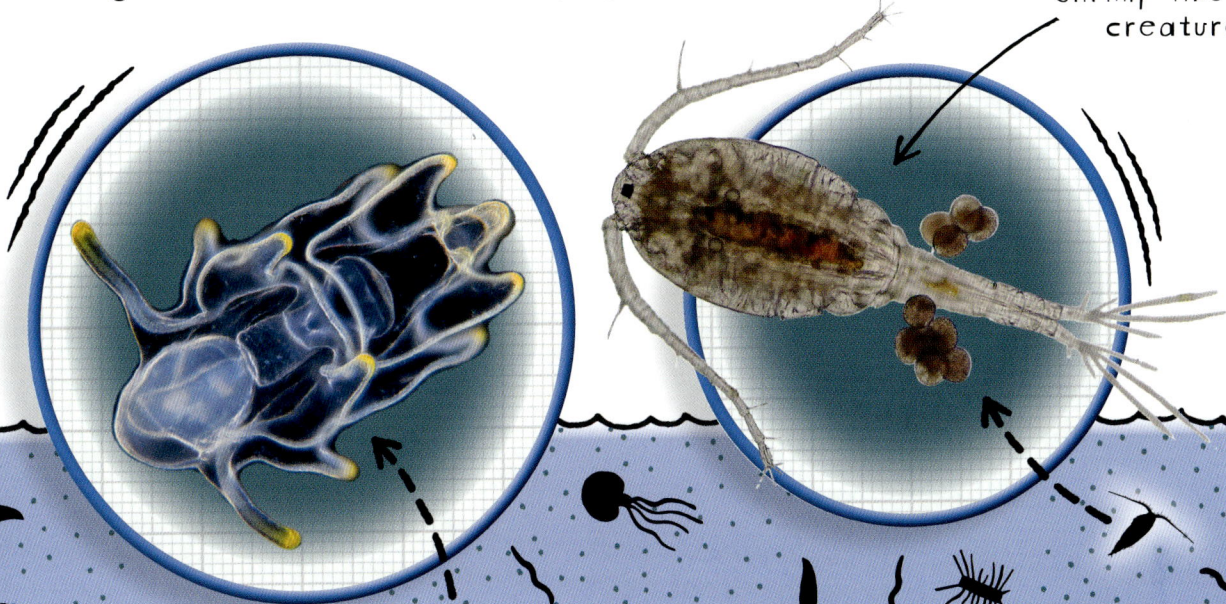

Baby sea star

Plankton power

Plankton are vital for sea life, because they provide food for other sea creatures.

YUM YUM!

Phytoplankton use sunlight to make food.

Zooplankton feed on phytoplankton.

Fish, jellyfish, crabs, sea urchins and other small sea creatures eat zooplankton.

Small sea creatures become prey for larger fish, sharks, whales, seals, penguins and squid.

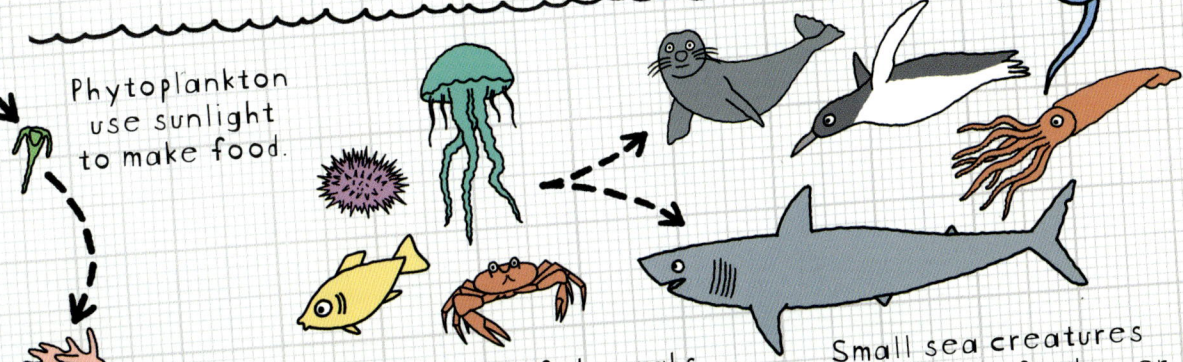

The soil is alive!

Soil might not seem all that interesting at first glance. But take a closer look, and it's bursting with life …

One handful of soil contains more living creatures (more than 50 billion) than the number of humans on Earth (not even 8 billion)!

Tiny creatures don't just live in the soil – they are actually part of it, and make it healthy.

Billions of bacteria

Soil is full of single-celled bacteria, which do several useful jobs:

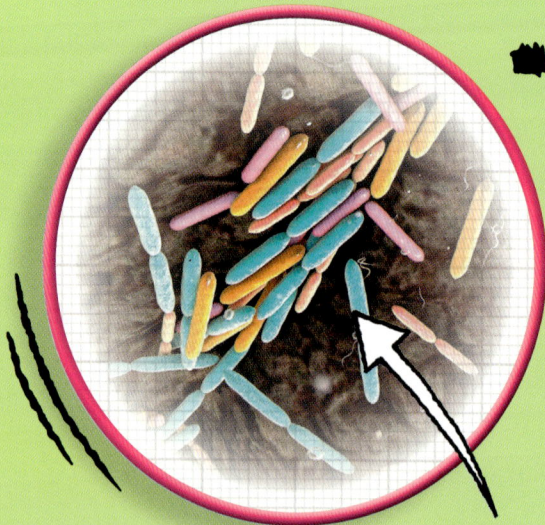

- Some feed on bits of dead plants and animals, breaking them down into nutrients (food chemicals) for plants and other soil life.

- Some slowly dissolve rocks and minerals, adding them to the soil too.

- Others take in nitrogen gas from the air and release it into the soil, where plants use it to help them grow.

Soil bacteria

Hairy fungi

Fungi in the soil form hair-like threads called hyphae. They hold soil together, and also grow around plant roots, where they help plants to soak up nutrients.

Hyphae →

16

Weeny worms

As well as bigger earthworms, soil is full of tiny nematode worms. They spread nutrients through the soil as they move around.

Nematode worm

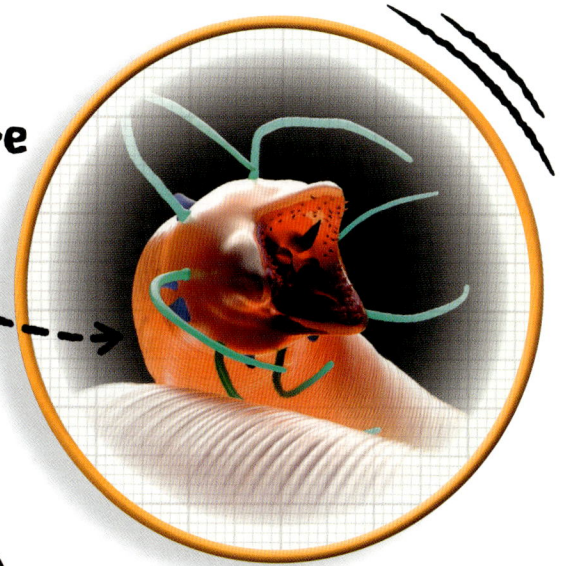

Boing!

Springtails are miniature creepy-crawlies, found mostly in the top layer of soil. If danger threatens, a springtail can flick its tail against the ground and spring away.

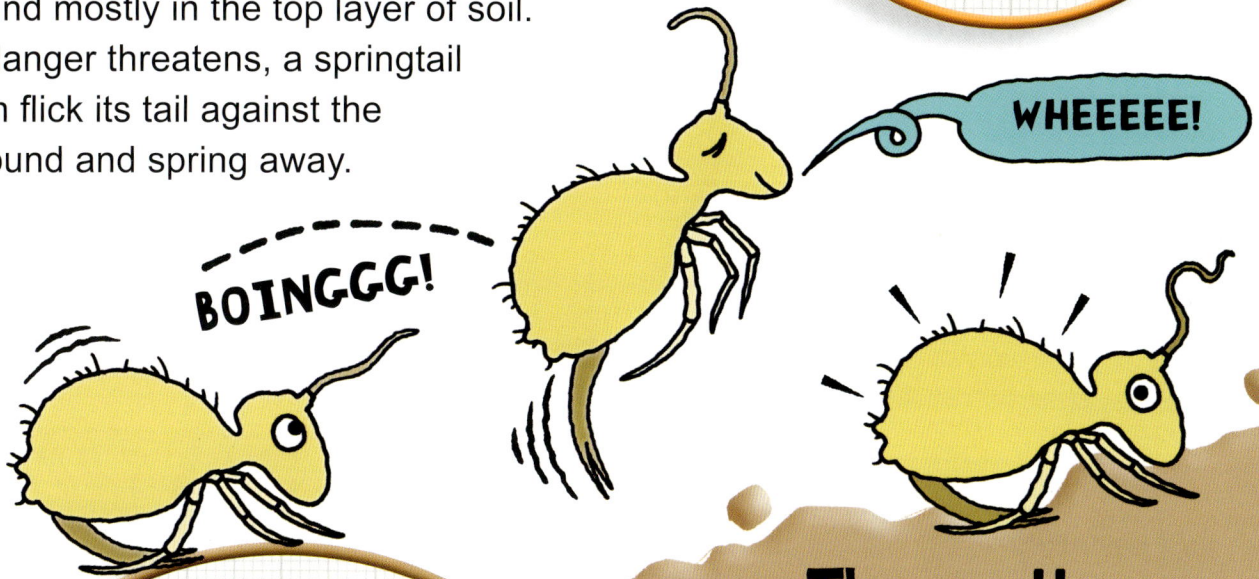

WHEEEEE!

BOINGGG!

And there's more!

We haven't even had space to include all these!

Soil mites

Minute millipedes

Microscopic flatworms

Pseudoscorpions

The smell of soil

The bacteria and other living things in soil give it its "earthy" smell. Farmers can tell if their soil is full of life by sniffing it!

MMMMM ... PERFECT!

Working together

Tiny creatures are in danger of being eaten, and it can be hard for them to get around too.

So, some microscopic creatures live together in groups – and the groups can be enormous!

Coral cities

Coral reefs in the sea are made out of a hard material similar to sea shell. Some reefs are so big they can be seen from space, but the animals that build them are tiny! They're called coral polyps, and they live in groups, or colonies.

Corals are linked by a layer of living cells. It builds the skeleton, and lets the polyps share food.

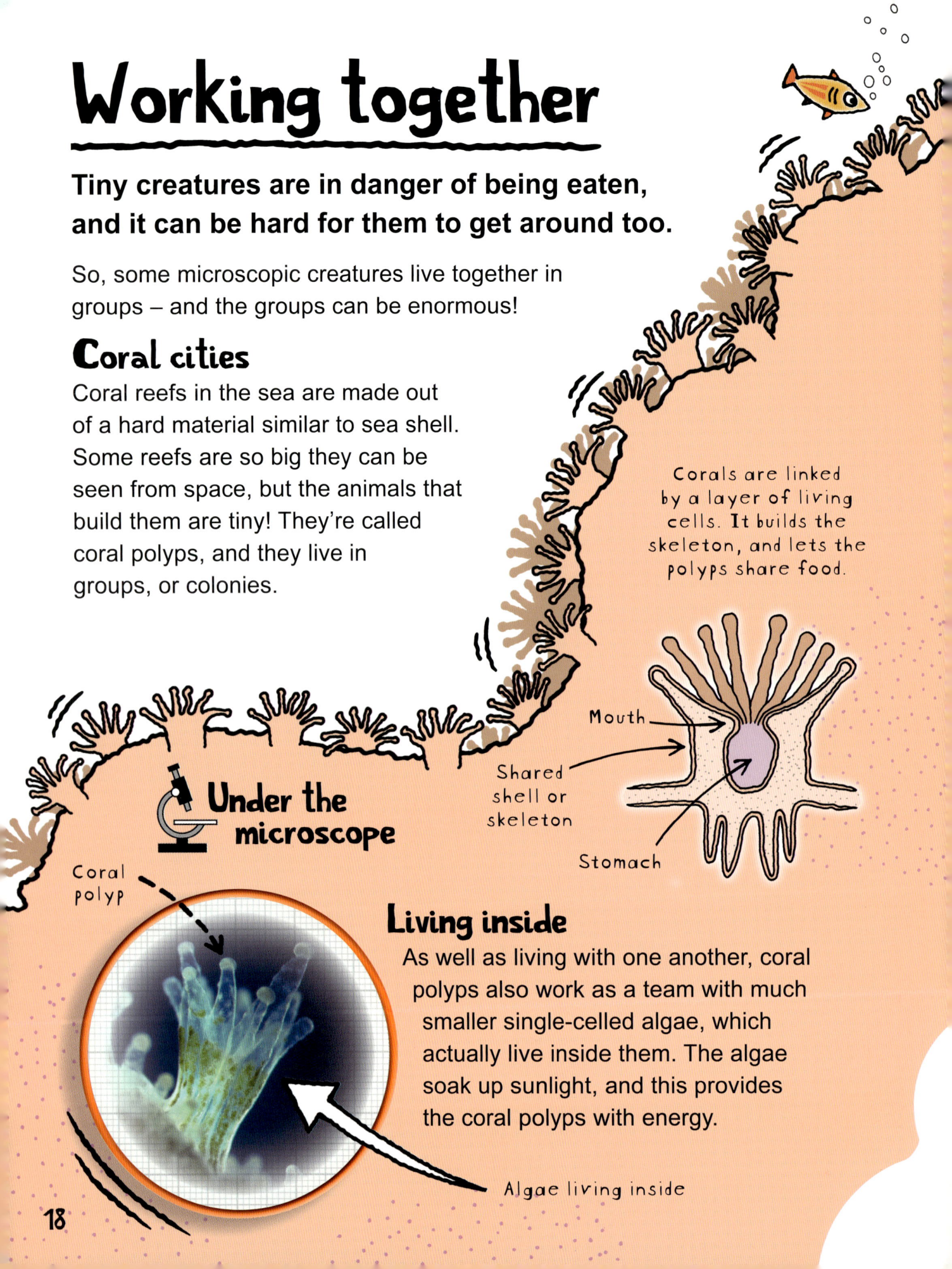

Mouth

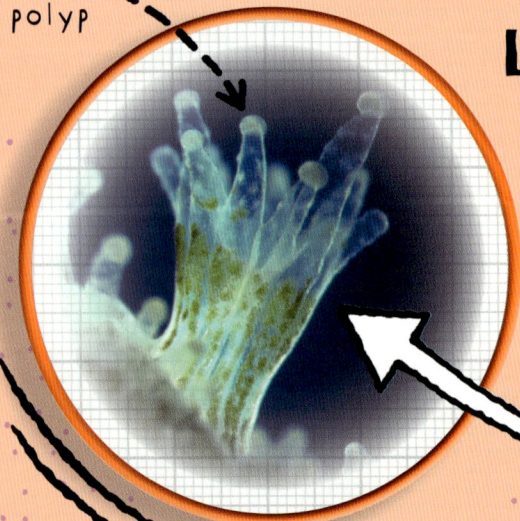

Shared shell or skeleton

Stomach

Under the microscope

Coral polyp

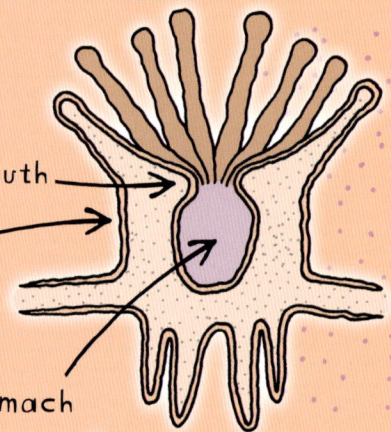

Living inside

As well as living with one another, coral polyps also work as a team with much smaller single-celled algae, which actually live inside them. The algae soak up sunlight, and this provides the coral polyps with energy.

Algae living inside

Giant sea tube

Here's another type of colony, a giant pyrosome. It's a huge tube up to 18 m long, made up of tiny creatures called zooids. They feed on plankton as the pyrosome drifts along. They can also glow with light.

A close-up view of the zooids

Slithering slime

Some types of single-celled microorganisms live on their own most of the time – but can sometimes form a colony held together by gooey slime. The slimy blob, called a slime mould, can creep around looking for food!

This type of slime mould, *Fuligo septica*, is also known as "dog vomit"!

WAS THAT YOU?!

Parasites

A parasite lives on or inside another living thing, and uses it for food. Not all parasites are tiny, but a lot are. After all, living in or on another living thing is the perfect way to survive if you're very small.

Parasites on animals

Cat with an itchy ear? It could have ear mites! These tiny spider-like parasites live inside the ears of cats, dogs and other animals, where they nibble on earwax and dead skin.

ITCH! ITCH!

In fact, almost all animals have mites, lice, fleas or other parasites that will live on them if they get a chance.

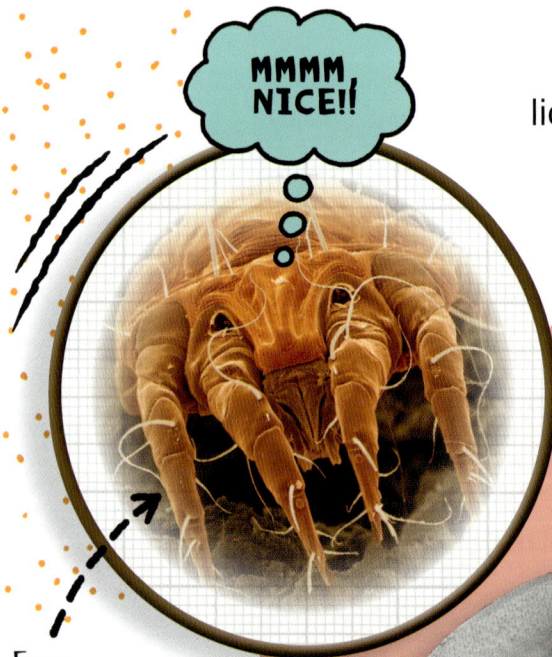

MMMM NICE!!

Ear mite

Under the microscope

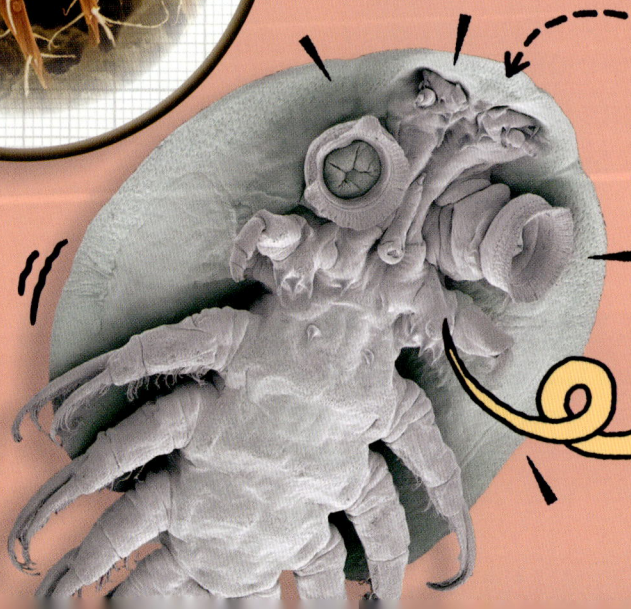

This freaky face belongs to a fish louse. They latch on to a fish's skin and suck its blood.

WHO ARE YOU CALLING FREAKY?!

Parasites on plants

Plants have parasites too, such as leaf miners. Several types of insect are leaf miners. They lay their eggs on leaves. When the baby hatches out, it lives inside the leaf, hollowing out a tunnel as it munches its way around.

A leaf miner baby

CHOMP! CHOMP!

Parasites on parasites!

There are even parasites that live on other parasites. They're called hyperparasites.

One example is the bat fly, a type of wingless fly that lives on a bat and sucks its blood. Besides being parasites, bat flies themselves can have a parasitic fungus living on them.

URGH, I'VE GOT A GROSS BAT FLY!

Bat

Bat fly

Fungus

OH NO, I'VE GOT AN ITCHY FUNGUS!

Am I safe?

Could tiny parasites be living on you too? YES! Step this way to take a look.

Living on humans

You are not alone! You share your body with trillions of tiny living things, who use it as a warm, cosy, all-you-can-eat hotel.

Gut bacteria

Your guts, or intestines, are the tubes where your body takes in nutrients and turns waste into poo. Bacteria living inside the intestines help your body to digest food, while taking a share for themselves.

Under the microscope

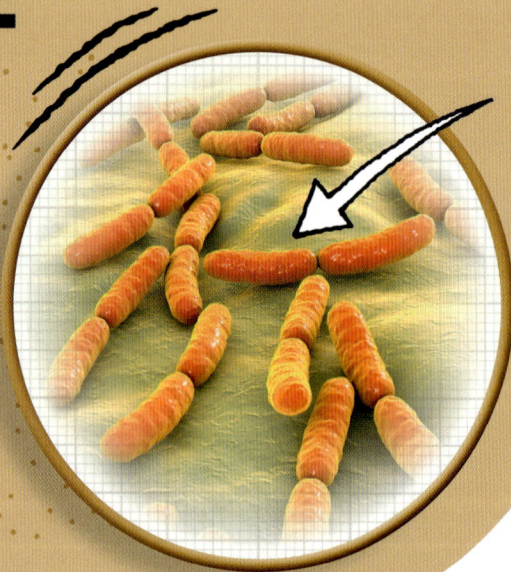

Over 30 TRILLION bacteria live in your guts at any one time! Luckily, they're extremely small – only about 2 μm across.

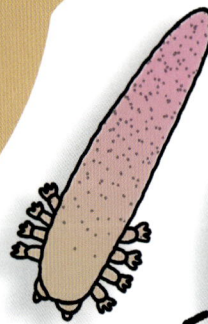

HUMAN HOTEL

We live on your face!

Meanwhile, more microscopic creatures live on your skin. These demodex mites, for example, live around hair follicles, where hairs grow out of the skin – especially eyelash and eyebrow hairs. They feed on sebum, or skin oil.

Foot fungus

Athlete's foot is an itchy fungus that can grow between your toes. It looks like this.

(If you ever have it, don't worry – a special cream can get rid of it!)

On your head!

And most people have been visited by another teeny-weeny creepy-crawly – the head louse. This microscope photo shows a head louse posing for a portrait while clinging to a human hair!

They're in your house too!

Micro-creatures live all over your home – such as book lice that chew on old books, and fungi growing on damp bathroom tiles.

There are also millions of dust mites, who love to eat the old, dead skin cells found in household dust.

I LOVE DUSTY CARPETS!

Don't Panic!

You might be feeling a bit itchy now, but don't worry! Most of these tiny parasites are not harmful.

23

Tiny life cycles

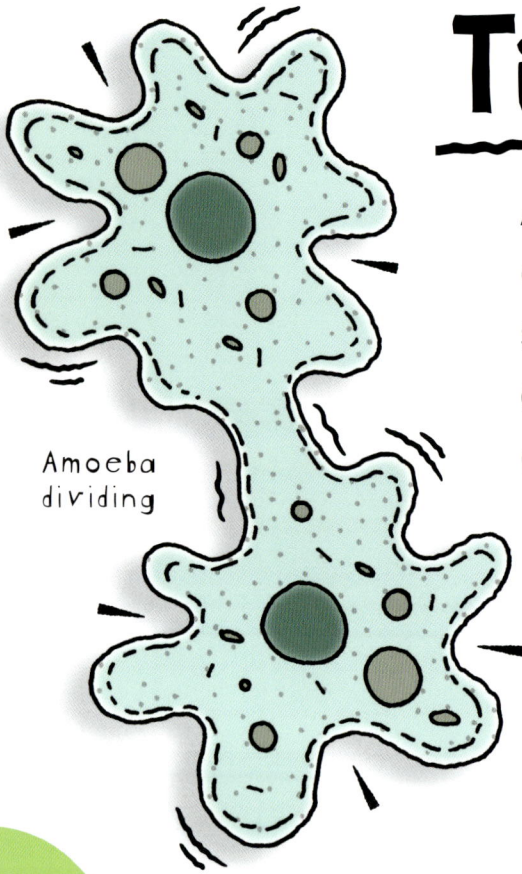

All living things reproduce, or make copies of themselves, so their species can carry on existing. Here's how microscopic creatures do it …

Amoeba dividing

One becomes two

For really tiny living things with only one cell, the simplest way to reproduce is to split in two. An amoeba is a single-celled, animal-like microorganism. To reproduce, it grows bigger, makes copies of all its parts, then divides into two.

Baby buds

Budding is another way of having babies. The adult living thing grows a "bud" on its body, which turns into a baby, then breaks off. Some corals, tiny flatworms, and bread yeast reproduce this way. Tiny Wolffia duckweed plants (see page 8) can do it too.

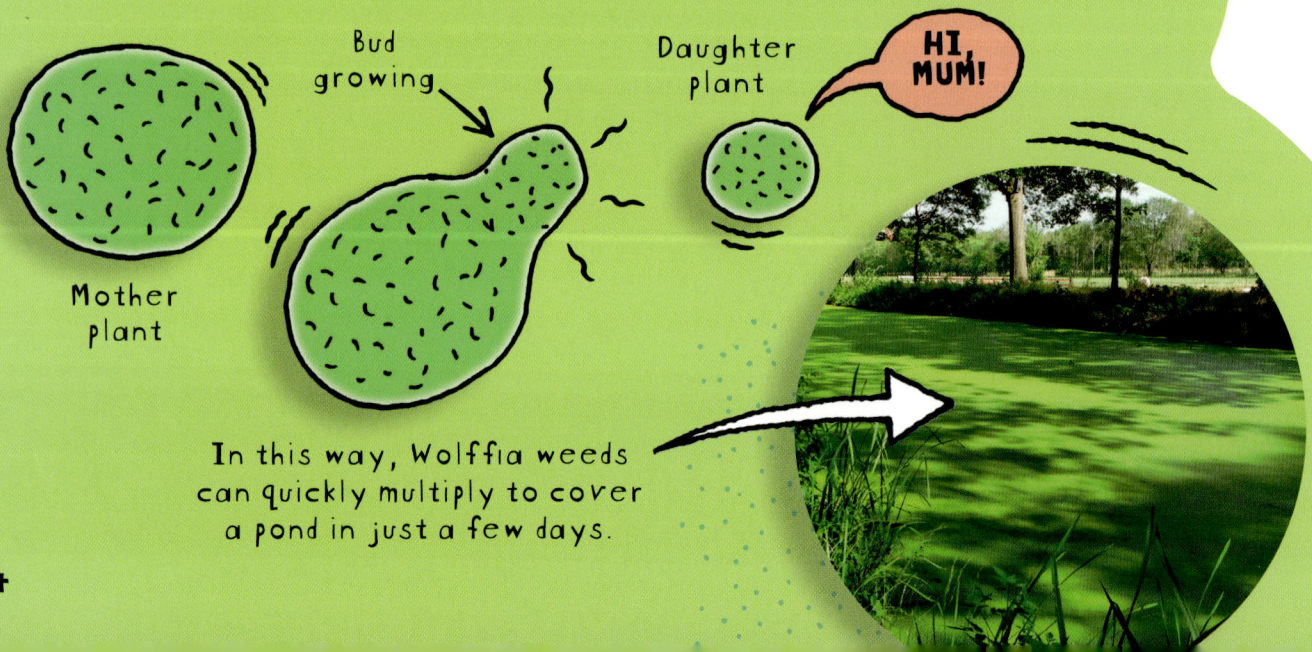

Mother plant

Bud growing

Daughter plant

HI MUM!

In this way, Wolffia weeds can quickly multiply to cover a pond in just a few days.

Eggs and babies

Some tiny creatures lay eggs – nematode worms, dust mites and tardigrades, for example.

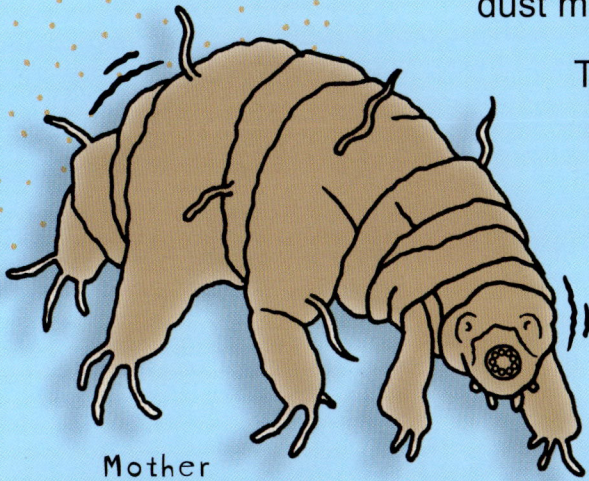

Tardigrades shed their skin as they grow bigger, and it comes in handy when a female tardigrade lays her eggs. She uses her old skin as a nest, laying her eggs safely inside it.

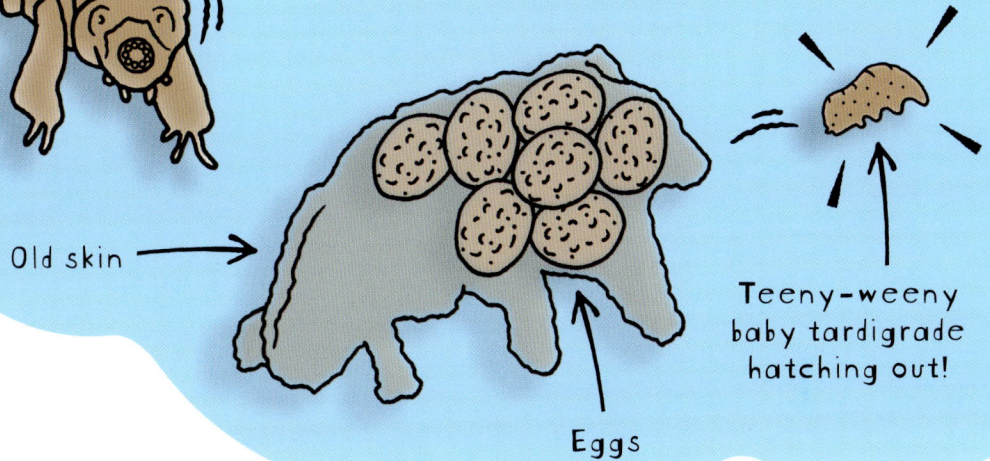

Mother tardigrade

Old skin

Teeny-weeny baby tardigrade hatching out!

Eggs

Invisible eggs

Some living things are not microscopic, but their eggs are. Parasitic threadworms can spread from person to person when their tiny eggs get on to people's hands or clothes.

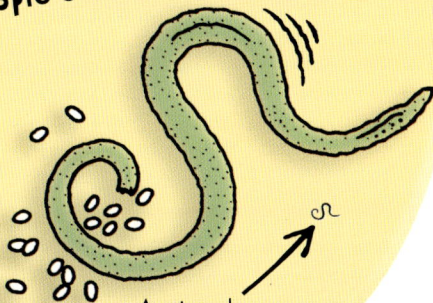

Actual size

Plant pollen

Many plants make tiny pollen grains that contain cells for making their seeds. Under a microscope, you can see the amazing shapes of different types of pollen.

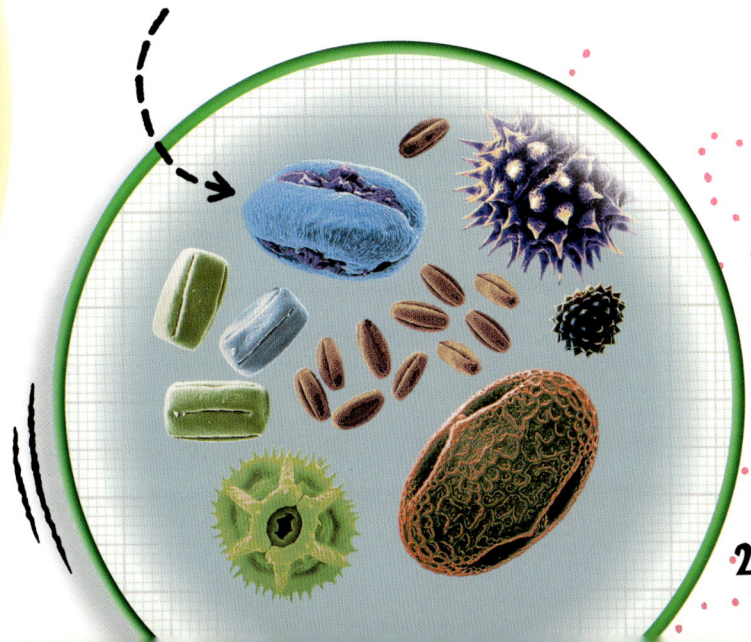

Record-breakers

You've already met the smallest plant, insect and spider. Here are some more vanishingly small record-holders!

Smallest snail

The world's smallest snail, called *Angustopila dominikae*, was only discovered in 2015, living in the soil in southern China. It's just 0.86 mm across – small enough to fit through the eye of a needle.

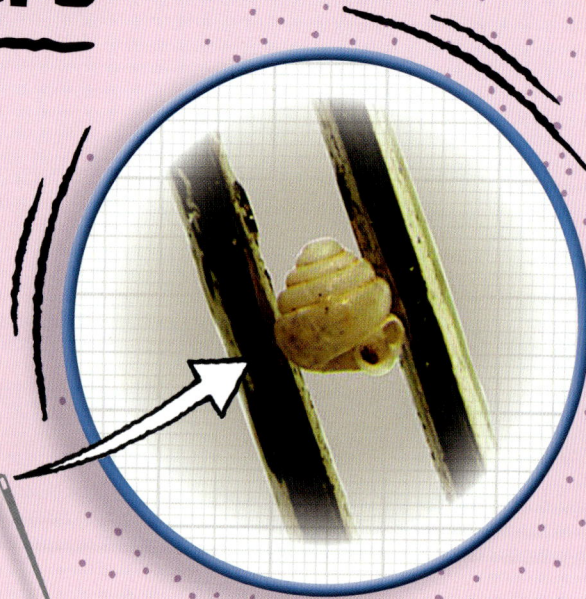

Weeniest worm

The smallest worm of them all is a type of nematode worm, Greeffiella, at about 80 µm long (about 0.08 mm). They live in slimy mud at the bottom of the sea and are totally transparent.

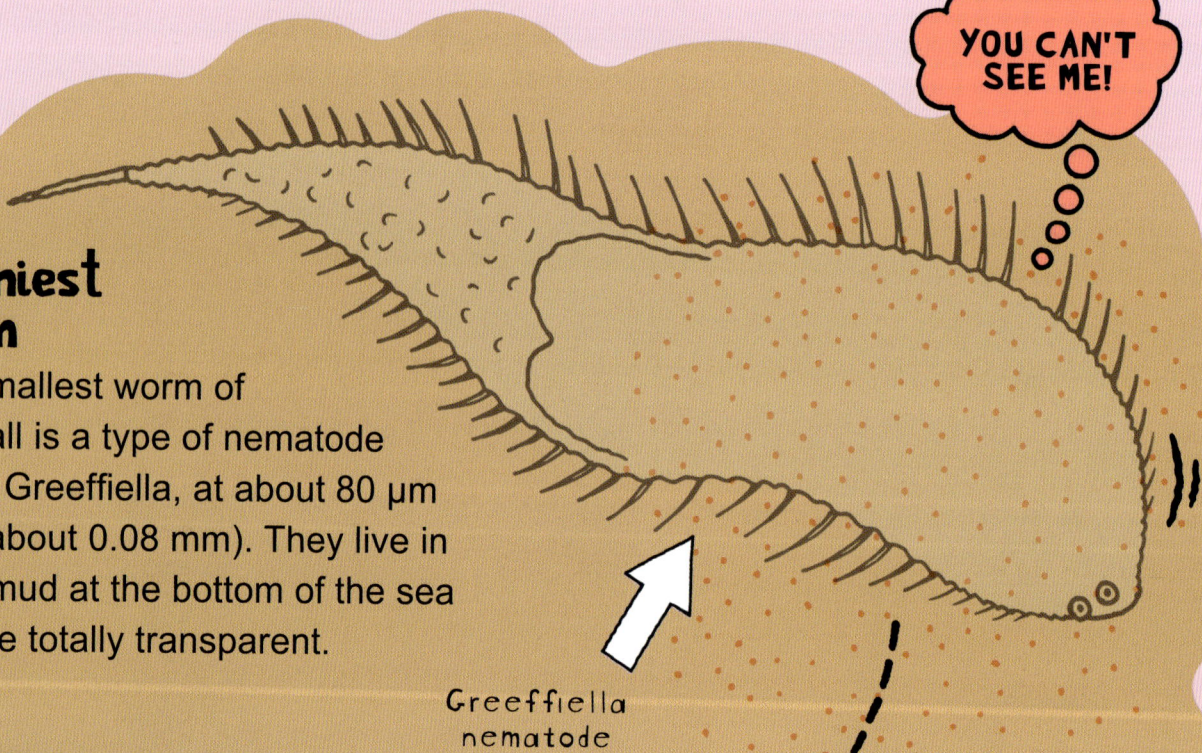

YOU CAN'T SEE ME!

Greeffiella nematode

mm

1

2

Tiniest mite

Several mite species could claim the title of tiniest mite, at less than 0.1 mm or 100 μm long. Here's one of them caught on camera, the apple rust mite. They chomp on apple tree leaves and fruit, causing a headache for apple farmers.

APPLES ... YUM YUM!

Apple rust mite

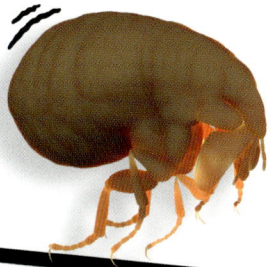

1 mm

Teeniest flea

The chigoe flea is the smallest flea, at just under 1 mm across. It can be a big nuisance, though, as the female burrows into human skin to lay eggs, causing itching and pain.

OUCH!

Chigoe fleas often burrow into people's feet.

Mycoplasma

Smallest living thing of all!

If you don't count viruses (which don't have cells and are not always alive), the smallest living thing is the mycoplasma bacterium. It's only about one third of one μm wide. You could fit a row of 3,000 of them into one millimetre.

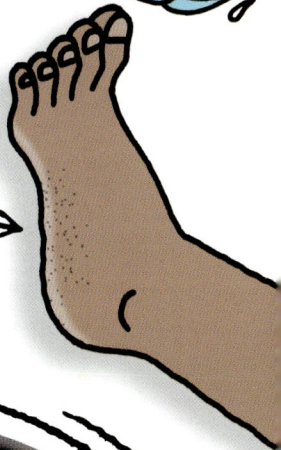

More to discover

By their nature, microscopic creatures are hard to see, and that makes them hard to find! So, we might find new, even smaller species in the future ...

How tiny?

This book is full of seriously small creatures, but although they are all tiny, some are bigger than others. Here are some of them shown to scale, so you can see their sizes compared to one another.

Micro measures

For measuring normal everyday things, we use centimetres, inches, metres or feet. But for much smaller things like bacteria and other microscopic creatures, scientists use the micron, or micrometre.

One micron is 1,000th of a millimetre.

So there are 1,000 microns in a millimetre... and 1 million microns in a metre.

The micron symbol is:

µm

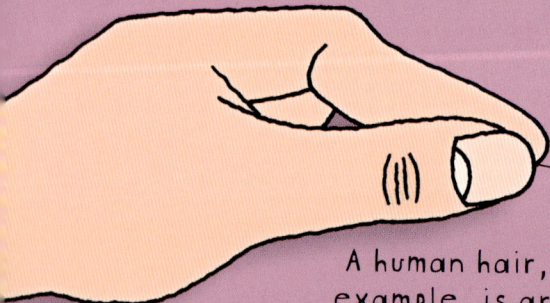

A human hair, for example, is around 80 µm thick.

Chlorella algae

Gut bacteria

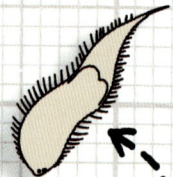
Greeffiella nematode

Pollen grain

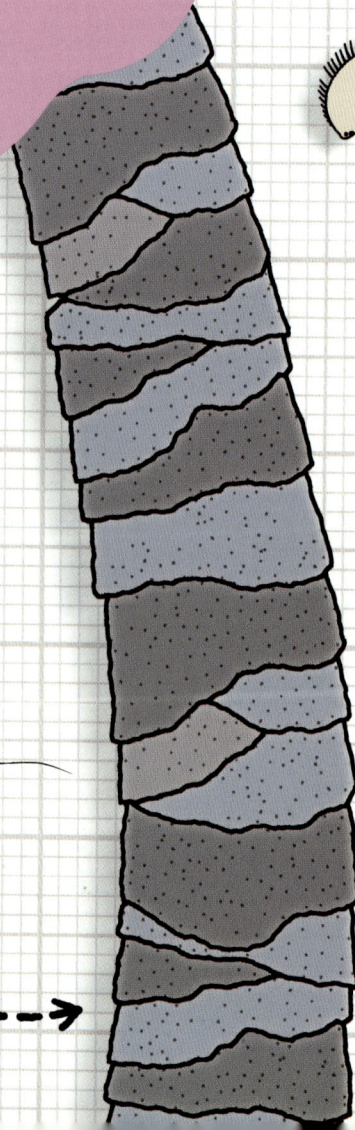

Jewel orchid seed

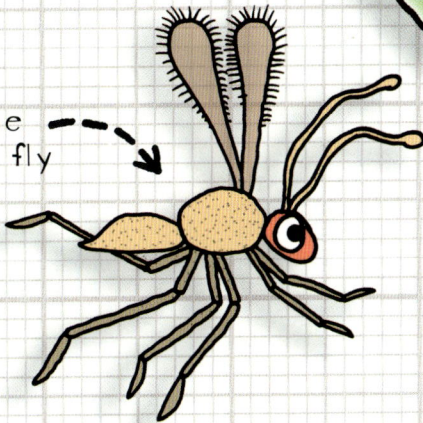
Male fairy fly

Wolffia plant

Diatom

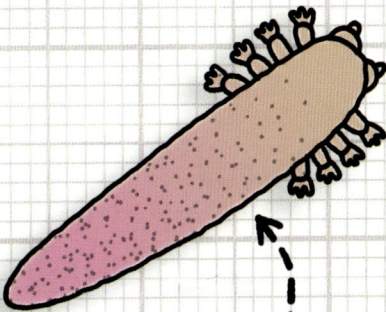
Eyelash mite

Mycoplasma bacterium

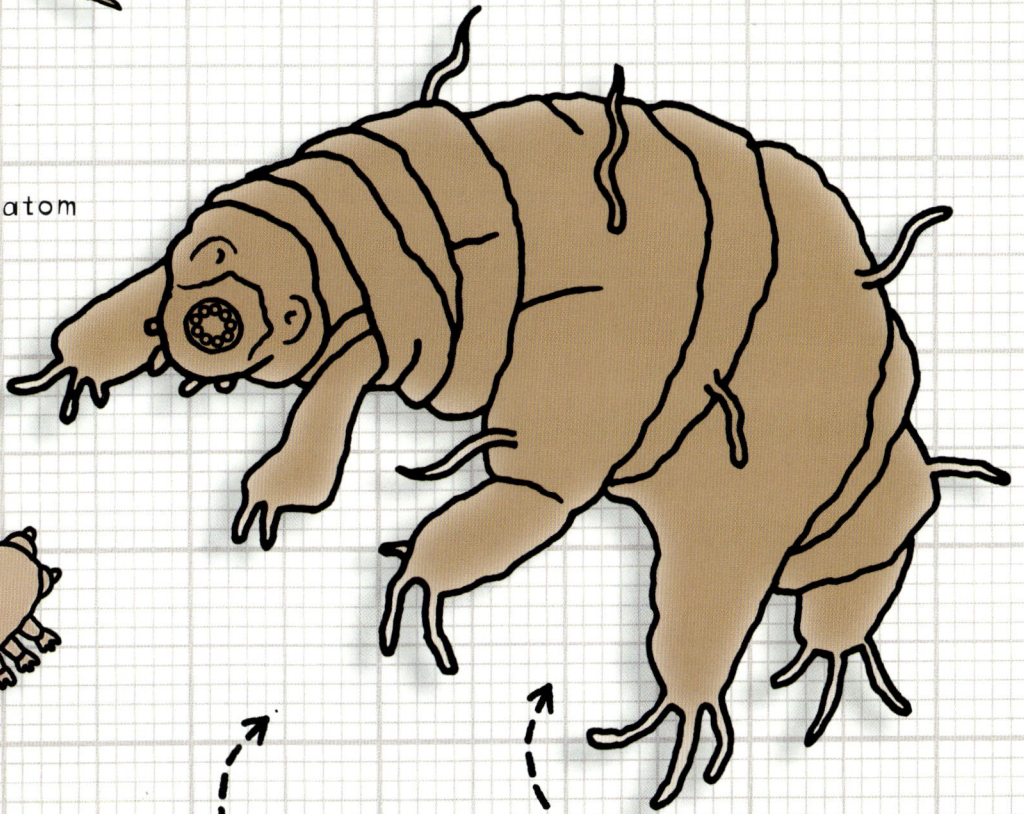
Tardigrade

Glossary

algae A type of living thing similar to plants, but often microscopic and single-celled.

amoeba A type of single-celled living thing that moves around and catches food.

archaea A type of single-celled living thing similar to bacteria.

athlete's foot A foot infection caused by a fungus, which gives you sore, flaky skin.

bacteria A type of very small, single-celled living thing.

bioluminescence The ability of a living thing to glow with its own light.

bud A type of baby living thing that grows from one side of its parent, then breaks off.

carbon dioxide A gas found in the air and released in some types of pollution, which contributes to global warming.

cells The tiny building blocks that make up living things.

coccolithophore A type of single-celled plankton found in the sea.

colony A group of living things such as bacteria or fungi that live together as a group.

copepod A tiny sea creature related to shrimps.

coral The hard material made by coral polyps as a protective shell.

coral polyps Tiny sea creatures that live in colonies and build layers of hard shell or coral.

daphnia Tiny shrimp-like water animals, also called water fleas.

diatom A type of single-celled algae with a hard outer covering.

dinoflagellate A type of single-celled water creature found in plankton.

evolve How species of living things gradually change over time.

fairy fly A very small wasp, and the smallest known type of insect.

flatworm A type of simple worm with a flat body.

flea A type of wingless insect that moves around by jumping.

fungi A group of living things that includes moulds, mushrooms and yeast.

gastrotrich A type of tiny worm-like water animal.

germs Tiny living things that can cause diseases in other living things.

global warming An increase in the Earth's average temperature caused by human activities.

hyphae The branching, root-like parts of a fungus.

lens A curved, clear piece of glass or other transparent material that bends light and can be used to magnify objects.

microbiology The study of microscopic living things.

micrometre Another name for a micron.

micron A tiny unit of measurement, one thousandth of a millimetre long.

microorganisms Very small living things, especially single-celled creatures such as bacteria and amoebae.

mite A tiny eight-legged animal related to spiders.

nematode worm A type of worm often found in water and soil, or living inside other animals.

nitrogen An element found in the air as a gas, and also as an important part of living things.

nutrients Chemicals that can be used as food by living things.

parasite A living thing that lives on or inside another living thing and takes its food from it.

photosynthesis The process plants use to turn water and carbon dioxide into food, using energy from sunlight.

phytoplankton Plankton that use photosynthesis to feed themselves, as plants do.

plankton A mass of tiny living things that drift around in water, especially in the sea, and provide food for other creatures.

pseudoscorpion A type of tiny animal related to spiders, with scorpion-like pincers.

pyrosome A large tube-shaped sea creature that is actually a colony of many tiny animals living as a group.

rotifer A type of tiny water animal.

single-celled Having only one cell.

slime mould A type of single-celled fungi that can live together in a group and behave like a larger living thing.

species A particular type of living thing.

springtail A type of very small animal related to insects, which can jump into the air.

tardigrade A tiny eight-legged animal found in all kinds of surroundings.

tun A dried-out ball that tardigrades can become to help them survive food and water shortages.

vacuum A space with nothing in it, not even air.

yeast A type of single-celled fungi.

zooids Tiny animals that live together in big groups or colonies, such as pyrosomes.

zooplankton Plankton that feed on other plankton.

Further information

Websites

www.amnh.org/explore/ology/microbiology
Games, info and activities on microorganisms from the American Museum of Natural History.

joyfulmicrobe.com/find-a-tardigrade
How to find a real-life tardigrade with a microscope, from the Joyful Microbe website.

www1.pbrc.hawaii.edu/microangela
Amazing microscope pictures of all kinds of tiny creatures and cells.

askabiologist.asu.edu/explore/plankton
All about plankton, with a picture gallery, from Ask a Biologist.

Books

Unseen Worlds: Real-Life Microscopic Creatures Hiding All Around Us
By Hèlène Rajcak and Damien Laverdunt (What on Earth Books, 2019)

Tiny Monsters: The Strange Creatures That Live On Us, In Us and Around Us
By Steve Jenkins and Robin Page (HMH Books for Young Readers, 2020)

Microbe Wars: Humanity's Biggest Battles with the World's Smallest Life-Forms
By Gill Arbuthnott and Marianna Madriz (Templar Publishing, 2021)

All in a Drop: How Antony van Leeuwenhoek Discovered an Invisible World
by Lori Alexander and Vivien Mildenberger (HMH Books, 2021)

The Micro World of Dust Mites and Other Microscopic Creatures
By Melissa Mayer (Capstone Press, 2022)

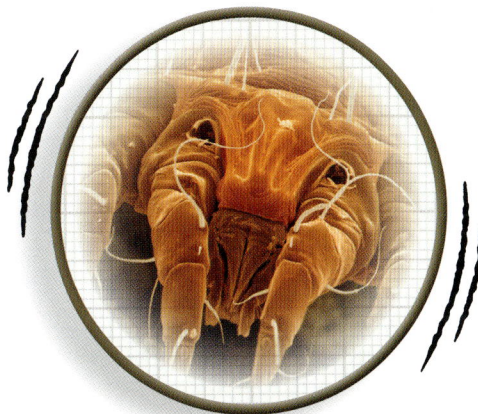

Index

Tiny Science titles:

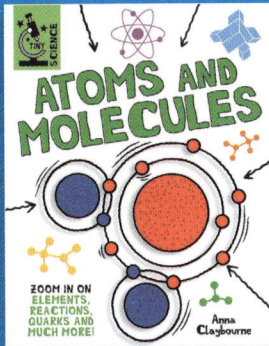

ATOMS AND MOLECULES

ZOOM IN ON ELEMENTS, REACTIONS, QUARKS AND MUCH MORE!

Anna Claybourne

HB 978 1 5263 1791 9
PB 978 1 5263 1792 6

WHAT'S EVERYTHING MADE OF?
ATOMS IN CLOSE-UP
MAKING MOLECULES
IT'S ELEMENTARY!
MILLIONS OF MATERIALS
BOOM!
HOT AND COLD
HOW DO WE KNOW?
SPLITTING THE ATOM
THERE THEY ARE!
ATOMIC INVENTIONS
WHAT ARE SUBATOMIC PARTICLES MADE OF?
HOW TINY?

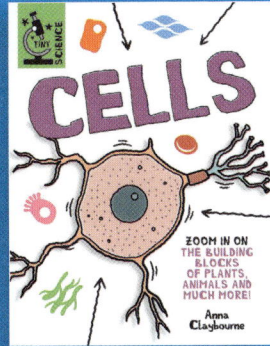

CELLS

ZOOM IN ON THE BUILDING BLOCKS OF PLANTS, ANIMALS AND MUCH MORE!

Anna Claybourne

HB 978 1 5263 1783 4
PB 978 1 5263 1784 1

WHAT ARE CELLS?
HOW MANY CELLS?
TYPES OF CELL
PARTS OF A CELL
HOW CELLS WORK
SMALL AND SIMPLE
PLANT CELLS
ANIMAL CELLS
FUNGI CELLS
HUMAN BODY CELLS
MAKING MORE CELLS
WORKING TOGETHER
HOW TINY?

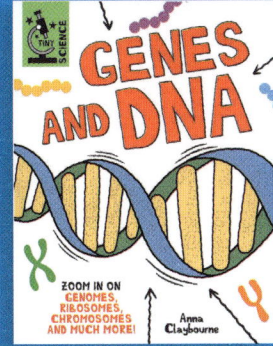

GENES AND DNA

ZOOM IN ON GENOMES, RIBOSOMES, CHROMOSOMES AND MUCH MORE!

Anna Claybourne

HB 978 1 5263 1785 8
PB 978 1 5263 1786 5

WHAT ARE GENES AND DNA?
THE TREE OF LIFE
PASSING IT ON
HUMAN GENES
WHAT'S IN YOUR GENES?
INSIDE CELLS
WHAT GENES DO
THE GENE CODE
DNA DISCOVERY
DNA DETECTIVES
CHANGING GENES
GENE INVENTIONS
HOW TINY?

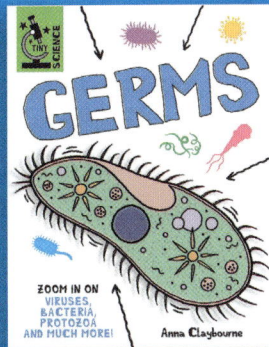

GERMS

ZOOM IN ON VIRUSES, BACTERIA, PROTOZOA AND MUCH MORE!

Anna Claybourne

HB 978 1 5263 1730 8
PB 978 1 5263 1731 5

WHAT ARE GERMS?
GERMS AND DISEASES
TYPES OF GERM
BACTERIA
VIRUSES
FUNGI
PROTOZOA
INFECTION!
PASSING IT ON
FIGHTING OFF GERMS
THE WAR ON GERMS
IT'S NOT JUST US!
HOW TINY?

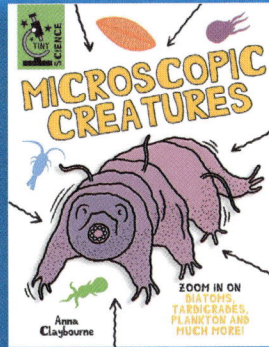

MICROSCOPIC CREATURES

ZOOM IN ON DIATOMS, TARDIGRADES, PLANKTON AND MUCH MORE!

Anna Claybourne

HB 978 1 5263 1787 2
PB 978 1 5263 1788 9

TINY LIFE
A WHOLE NEW WORLD
TINY PLANTS
TINY ANIMALS
TINY BUT TOUGH TARDIGRADES
UNDERWATER WORLD
THE SOIL IS ALIVE!
WORKING TOGETHER
PARASITES
LIVING ON HUMANS
TINY LIFE CYCLES
RECORD BREAKERS
HOW TINY?

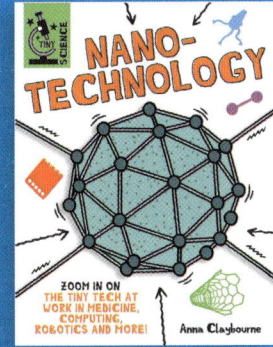

NANO-TECHNOLOGY

ZOOM IN ON THE TINY TECH AT WORK IN MEDICINE, COMPUTING, ROBOTICS AND MORE!

Anna Claybourne

HB 978 1 5263 1793 3
PB 978 1 5263 1794 0

TINY TECHNOLOGY
SMALLER AND SMALLER
NANO NATURE
WORKING WITH ATOMS
MINI MATERIALS
NANO CLEAN-UP
NANOMEDICINE
NANOCOMPUTERS
THE NANOBOTS ARE COMING!
SAVING THE PLANET
WHAT COULD POSSIBLY GO WRONG?
FUTURE NANOTECH
HOW TINY?

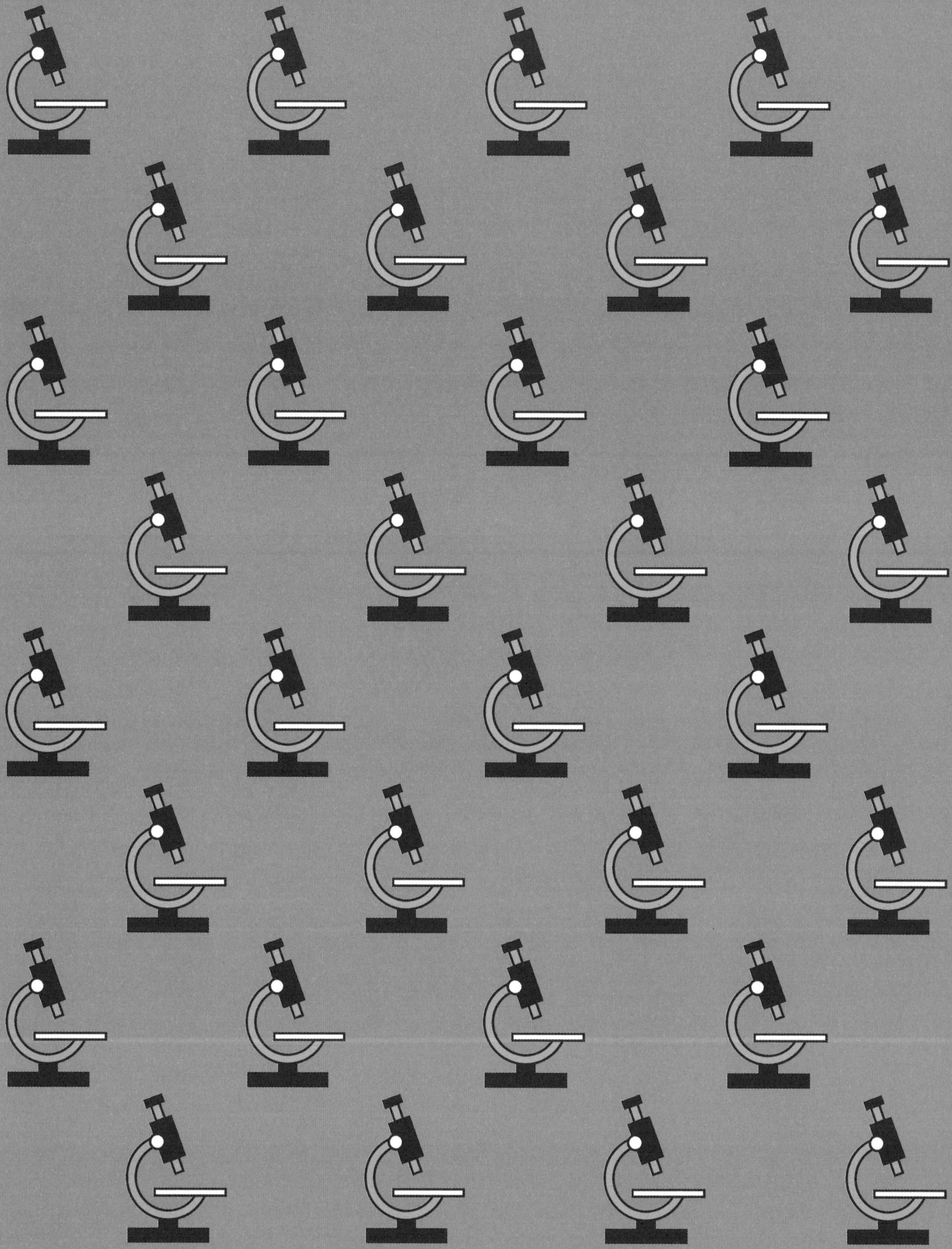